Jesus Christ
Sermon on the Mount

By Jerry L. Mercer

Contents

Introduction

God speaks to us all. Our responsibility is to listen and to respond. The salvation of clerks, executives, mechanics, teachers, bankers, salespeople—indeed, the salvation of everyone—depends on a deep desire to hear God's word and the will to do it.

Recognizing our responsibility to listen to God and to respond to God serves as a good introduction to our study. For surely the greatest message to which we can ever listen is the one Jesus speaks to us in the Sermon on the Mount and with it the Sermon on the Plain.

John, the author of the Fourth Gospel, especially understood belief in Jesus Christ to mean more than merely recognizing that Jesus lived or having some sentimental appreciation of his exemplary life and his ethical teachings. To believe in the sense of the gospel is to commit our lives to Jesus Christ as Savior so that we do what he says.

However, this is easier to say than to do. Many who call themselves Christian do not listen to what Jesus says, much less live in obedience to his teaching. Even in the church Jesus often is more admired than followed.

To be a listener is to be a disciple, since disciples are really students. And good students listen to their teacher. The church believes that Jesus is the greatest teacher. Because of the Resurrection, the teachings of Jesus are eternal. As drastically as times have changed from the time Jesus lived until now, the call to discipleship is the same today as then: "Follow me" (Matthew 4:19).

To follow Jesus we must first hear him. We hear him correctly when we willingly set aside *what we want him to say* and listen to *what he actually says*. But listening to Jesus is risky business. Those who have followed him through the years have learned that his words are at first painful and then soothing. They are painful when they tear at the illusions we have about ourselves and

God. They are soothing when they fill our hearts with acceptance and love.

John Wesley was particularly fond of the Sermon on the Mount. Wesley believed that through this sermon Jesus taught the true way to life everlasting, "the royal way which leads to the Kingdom." This is certainly true. It is "the royal way" to the Kingdom now and in the future.

As we learn from Scripture, we enter the Kingdom by repentance and faith nourished and enlarged through love. The Kingdom serves as the driving force and final destiny of the church. In this study we follow Jesus along the royal way in search of the Kingdom.

The Sermon on the Mount can be divided into six sections. These sections make up the six chapters in this book. Together the sections outline the royal way to the Kingdom. As we shall see, the particular concerns of the Sermon on the Plain from Luke's Gospel fit into the larger concerns of Matthew's report of the Sermon on the Mount. For that reason the Sermon on the Mount from Matthew will be the main text with references to Luke. This book is designed to be read *along with* the Scripture texts for each chapter of the book.

You will benefit most from this study if you do the following:

1. Read carefully the Scripture texts for each chapter. Try to connect the texts with the chapter title.

2. Meditate on words or ideas that impress themselves on you during your reading.

3. Pray to the Holy Spirit to teach you as you read.

4. Read the chapter. Pause for reflection and prayer when you sense the need.

5. Underline or note the parts of each chapter that call you to a level of discipleship beyond where you are now. Use these insights for meditation and prayer.

Above all, commit your way to Christ's way. His is indeed "the royal way" that leads to life. Now come and follow him.

Jerry L. Mercer, Writer

1

A Joyful Way

The royal way is a joyful way. In Matthew 5:1-16 Jesus described for his listeners persons who walk that joyful way.

Paul wrote that one of the fruits of the Holy Spirit is joy (Galatians 5:22-23). Every person whose life has been changed by Jesus Christ knows that this is true. Life in Jesus Christ is a song of love and gratitude. Explaining just what happens is difficult, but this happy presence of Jesus Christ with us and in us is a common experience. This joyous love of God makes our life glorious and new.

Francis of Assisi was a man who could not keep his joy and exuberance contained. I have read much about Francis, and like many others I have been overwhelmed by him. This Italian saint literally was consumed by the desire to love God. He gave himself to God with a joyous abandon that would make the most ardent lovers jealous. Francis's own writings and those about him reflect a sense of joy that is hard to believe. He stripped himself of ambition and possessions in order to be as free as possible to pursue his one dream—to love God perfectly.

For many of us a person like Francis of Assisi seems too good to be true. He is like a fairy tale, and perhaps much of what has been written about him is more fantasy than fact. Yet if you strip the tales about him as bare as you can, what remains is a vision of life higher than most of us live, exhibiting a joy deeper than most of us attain.

You see, Francis, son of Bernardone, had been captured by Christ. Francis was led to experience the depths of love and contentment through renunciation and self-denial. But all of his austere practices were never ends in themselves. They were done to enable him to love God more perfectly. And his was no private faith. Anyone familiar with his story knows that Francis's life was a reaching out in love to every person's needs.

In Jesus Christ Francis discovered a sense of acceptance and a personal destiny of loving service unmatched by any purely secular job or position. Of course, we all know that money cannot buy love, prestige cannot provide peace, and power cannot guarantee a meaningful life. But this is why Jesus came, to teach Francis and us that there is a way—a "royal way"—to a life of unparalleled blessedness and joy.

This blessedness, this joyous life, in no way depends on who you are or where you are from or what you have. It is a life lived in the spiritual fountain of youth, even when it must be lived in pain, isolation, and rejection.

The first characteristic we see in the biblical description of this royal way to the kingdom of God is that it is deeply joyful. The Greek word translated "blessed" in Matthew 5:1-16 means happy, fortunate, joyful. This joy that Jesus described comes as a sheer gift of God. It is given to those persons who more than anything else want to follow Christ. We do not have to travel far with Jesus before we begin to see just how radical his way is for us.

Jesus' joy challenges typical social standards and programs. His joy calls us to question many values that our culture prizes highly. As far as Jesus is concerned, true happiness is more than having a successful business or enrolling in a good retirement program or owning an elegant home. The joy that Jesus provides puts our values in the heavens with God and in the gutters of human misery with the needy.

The joy Jesus brings is for those people who find that their best efforts to live meaningfully are frustrated and cut short. It is for those who can no longer kid themselves into thinking that happiness really will come if that job comes through, if they could just be independent, if they could just be beautiful. Jesus calls the frustrated, the anxious, and the tired to rejoice!

Having found that all your own best efforts leave you empty, you are ready to walk Jesus Christ's way to joy.

The day Jesus sat down to talk with his disciples and the crowd around him and spoke the words of the Sermon on the Mount was a day of liberation.

The people who heard Jesus that day were not very much different from us. They were oppressed by political threats over which they had no control. Some of them suffered great physical and emotional pain. Some of them were embarrassed by their social standing, destined by a type of caste system to a life of mediocrity at best. Many of them struggled with low self-esteem. Some felt the guilts of their sin. All who were faithfully religious were subject to many legalisms and restrictions. The law of Moses, intended to set them free, had become a burden that condemned them.

Before Jesus on this day sat a large group of sinners, ordinary people hoping against hope that just maybe this teacher from the north country might be another Moses. And he was—and is! But the freedom he offers is not a freedom according to earthly expectations but a freedom according to heavenly expectations. He offers us his free and joyful way in the Sermon on the Mount and the Sermon on the Plain.

John Wesley believed that the eight Beatitudes spoken by Jesus in Matthew 5:1-16 are a series of steps, each more demanding than the last. If we follow them, these steps will lead us to the Kingdom, Wesley taught. In one sense this Kingdom is still ahead of us, in our future. We anticipate this coming Kingdom. But the Kingdom is not just a reality way out there ahead of us. In a real sense the Kingdom is here among us now.

John Wesley also believed that the Beatitudes describe the experiences of those who are actually living in the first flush of the Kingdom. You see, the Scripture teaches that the Kingdom made its appearance in Jesus Christ. This Kingdom manifests itself in spiritual freedom here and now, even though the best is yet to be.

In our present lives, as Paul suggested, we see through a darkly colored glass; but the time is coming when we shall see clearly (1 Corinthians 13:12). Nevertheless, we can experience the freedom and joy of the kingdom of God every day as we live the way Jesus Christ shows us.

Therefore, we experience two dimensions to the kingdom of God.

We *live* now. We will *live more fully* later.

We *see* now. We will *see more clearly* later.

We *love* now. We will *love more fully* later.

The Kingdom is all of one piece—then and now, today and tomorrow. No wonder the Christian life is filled with joy. We have entered eternity!

In essence then, the Beatitudes show us what living in Christ for the glory of God means. They become an agenda by which we live every day. But remember: The Beatitudes are not some sort of program by which we work our way to heaven. We do not make ourselves acceptable to God by just living a good life. We are accepted when we reach out to God, depending only on God's love and mercy. The faithful life is a grace-filled life made possible only by God's free gift of God's love to us.

The Beatitudes in Luke's Gospel are different from those in Matthew. Luke, a physician, was concerned for the sick and the poor. So we are not surprised then when, in the Sermon on the Plain in Luke, Jesus speaks of God's love for the poor and God's judgment for the greedy rich. Luke's Gospel contains four blessings for the poor and four woes against the rich (Luke 6:20-26). In Matthew's account of the Sermon on the Mount are eight Beatitudes. We will consider the more restricted concerns of Luke within the larger concerns of Matthew.

The offer of the Kingdom by Jesus as emphasized by Matthew was a genuine offer. God wanted Israel to repent and return to God through the work of the Messiah, Jesus. Accepting this Kingdom, Israel would become a "light for the Gentiles" (Acts 13:47). But most people rejected the Messiah and refused the rule of God as Jesus proclaimed it.

Yet that was not the end of the matter. The Resurrection demonstrated that, regardless of the treatment God received at the hands of self-centered people, the Kingdom was still offered to all and the Kingdom would come! The Resurrection gives us confidence to believe that nothing can cancel out God's redeeming love. The Beatitudes are still essential as a guide to life if we are to live faithfully as God's people.

We can only hint at the power of the Beatitudes here. Each of us must reflect on each Beatitude and attempt to understand how each informs responsible Christian commitment. Let us look at the Beatitudes in turn and try to hear Jesus' voice speaking to us through them.

1. "Blessed are the poor in spirit, for theirs is the kingdom of heaven" (Matthew 5:3). Knowing our need of God is what being "poor in spirit" means. It is having a deep personal sense of one's need of God. Spiritual life begins and continues with this attitude.

These people who know their need of God are happy, because as needy ones they have found the Source of happiness.

2. "Blessed are those who mourn, for they shall be comforted" (Matthew 5:4). Since this saying on mourning follows that on poverty of spirit, its meaning must first apply to the spiritual life. The sense of failure and guilt we often feel when our selfish grasping for attention has been exposed by God is terrifying indeed. Surely we would despair were it not for God's assuring love poured into our hearts by the Holy Spirit.

This outpouring of God's love is a mystery of faith. We who are guilty are forgiven. We who seem lost without God are found by God. God's Spirit braces us, assures us of God's love, and releases us to love God and others—friends and enemies alike. No wonder joy follows our confession of sin.

3. "Blessed are the meek, for they shall inherit the earth" (Matthew 5:5). To be meek is to give oneself to God's will without question. Those who allow God to become the center of their lives experience an unbelievable freedom. Such focusing on God enables us to put all human experience, good and bad, in its proper perspective. In God, things are never as good as they will be or as bad as they seem.

The Israelites saw good earthly life as the blessing of God. In keeping with these kinds of hopes, the faith of the earthly church was for a resurrected body and a renewed earth. Death and pain, intruders into God's good plan for the world, would one day be put in their place. In times of nuclear threat this is a wonderful prospect.

4. "Blessed are those who hunger and thirst for righteousness, for they shall be satisfied" (Matthew 5:6). The note of urgency in seeking God is found throughout the Bible. This is true not only in discovering God's love for the first time but also in our daily attempts to do what pleases God. When we pray, worship, and serve God in the spirit of this saying, our lives are revolutionized.

Note that this teaching emphasizes the *search* for right living. Upright living comes from such single-mindedness. We are to be intentionally disciplined in our quest for the hallowed life. The satisfaction in doing God's will is our joy. We always get what we want when what we want is God.

5. "Blessed are the merciful, for they shall obtain mercy" (Matthew 5:7). True faith has no room for triumphalism or a holier-than-thou attitude. Christians give mercy freely because they recognize that they have freely received the mercy of God. We demonstrate mercy when we show compassion for someone who fails, when we show concern for someone who hurts, and when we give acceptance to someone who sins. This spirit of selfless mercy is absolutely essential for Christian community. Persons find joy in being merciful because of mercy's twofold effect: It helps the one giving it to grow in humility, and it helps the one receiving it to grow in dignity.

6. "Blessed are the pure in heart, for they shall see God" (Matthew 5:8). If people sought to be pure in heart toward God, think how wonderful living with one another would be!

A type of innocence goes along with purity of heart. It is the innocence that believes the best of other persons. It is the innocence that rejoices in the presence of other Christians. It is the innocence that identifies with anyone who suffers.

Such purity is deeply joyous because it enables us to live without malice toward others, even those who hurt us or misunderstand us. The reward of such people is the vision of God, "seeing" God with the eye of the pure heart.

7. "Blessed are the peacemakers, for they shall be called sons of God" (Matthew 5:9). At the base of self-hatred, family strife, and war are anger and resentment. The good news of our faith is that in Jesus Christ we can be reconciled with ourselves, with others, and with God. The gospel, the good news of Christ, brings peace.

Being a peacemaker means having a peaceful spirit.

11

It means creating an environment that promotes peace, and if necessary it means negotiating peace to the point of personal sacrifice. Peace is not just the absence of violence. In a hostile world that is being torn apart by selfishness, suspicion, and fear, the peaceful way of Christ is a joy-filled way.

8. "Blessed are those who are persecuted for righteousness' sake, for theirs is the kingdom of heaven" (Matthew 5:10). As Jesus was to learn first-hand, often the immediate reward for godliness is being insulted, persecuted, and falsely accused. But if and when that happens to us, the joy-filled way of Christ is not seeking revenge on our tormentors. Rather we are to turn to God and become saturated with God's love.

Christians live with hope. If our hope is temporarily shattered, that experience only drives us to a deeper trust in God's timing. All things are in God's hands, even our problems. We rest in the assurance of the justice of God and God's gift of eternal life. And the last promise is the same as the first: Theirs is the Kingdom of heaven. By loving God we will share in God's triumph.

A spiritual teacher once wrote that authentic Christianity is "simple, unreflecting obedience to the will of Christ." Francis of Assisi was described by a biographer as following Christ "without commentary." That is, he obeyed the will of God immediately and without deliberation.

Why do we Christians today find it so difficult to take Jesus at face value? If Francis had no particular agenda for the day, he would randomly stick his finger on a biblical text and do what that text said. Even John Wesley was not above the practice of "pricking" the Scripture on occasion in an attempt to see the will of God.

These stories make us smile, but they contain a great truth. Freedom is part of following Jesus' way, especially when we become convinced that his will is best for our lives.

Jesus told his disciples, "You are the salt of the

earth" (Matthew 5:13) and "You are the light of the world" (Matthew 5:14). These are vivid descriptions of the way Jesus' followers are supposed to live. Like salt they add flavor to life. They preserve righteousness, justice, and peace. Like light they shine in the darkness, and those groping around for a way out of the darkness see their light. Those who are lost are led to the Kingdom of light by those who know and follow Jesus.

These qualities of salt and light come from God, and God's people are to reflect them. They indicate something of the responsibility we have for the gospel in the world.

However, the salt and light sayings are also warnings. Salt can lose its properties and become a waste product, good for nothing except to be thrown away (Matthew 5:13). Also, we can take what light we have and hide it like a lamp under a bushel (Matthew 5:15-16).

Jesus calls us to simple obedience and absolute faithfulness. Therefore we should not be discouraged when we find Jesus questioning what we think and what we do. He searches our hearts in order to establish us in the faith. By the help of God, let us pledge fidelity to this Messiah. Let us make it our goal to follow him in the way of true joy.

2

A Deeper Way

The royal way is a deeper way. In Matthew 5:17-48 and Luke 6:27-36 Jesus talked about a way of life that goes beyond rules and regulations. We can almost hear the gasp of those listening to Jesus as he talked about the Law. "Think not that I have come to abolish the law and the prophets; I have come not to abolish them but to fulfil them" (Matthew 5:17).

To stand before the people as the embodiment of the prophetic hope of Israel was daring enough. But to say at the same time that the people were to hear Jesus, not the Law, as their final authority in matters of faith was simply unbelievable. Considering how important the Law was to the people of Jesus' day, it is easy to see why many people thought Jesus mad and why the Pharisees and scribes considered him a blasphemer.

Jesus knew the Law was only one way God had used to speak to God's people. In the earliest days of Israel, God made divine will known through gifted and sensitive leaders and teachers. Many of these people were especially important when the nation was threatened by enemies. They were called judges, and they led the people in battle and helped restore calm. As Israel grew as a nation, the written Law gradually rose to prominence. With this shift the role of the anointed leader began to decline. Emphasis shifted from God's leadership in the movement of history to keeping certain moral teachings in a fixed and timeless form. Over the years the Law became so central that the people seemed to exist to serve the Law, rather than the Law existing to help the people live upright lives. For all practical purposes in the minds of the people, the Law became the voice of God.

Jesus did not denounce the Law, although he rebuked some of its official teachers for teaching the Law wrongly. Jesus knew that the Law as originally intended was good. The early Hebrews received the Law as a gift from a caring God. The Psalms especially praise the Law. Jesus said the Law will not pass away. The Law is so important, Jesus said, that everything else—lands, possessions, families, the nation itself—is expendable by comparison. Indeed, "heaven and earth" are temporary, but not the Law!

The Hebrews did not keep the Law because they were afraid not to keep it. They kept it because keeping the Law pleased God, and that is what the Hebrews wanted more than anything else. But some of the prophets sensed the Law was being misused. For example, Jeremiah said the day was coming when the Law of God would no longer be written in books but on the hearts of people (Jeremiah 31:31-34).

Because the Law was written down and easily available, many people began to use it as a kind of security blanket. In the New Testament Paul tried to show that any privileged position the Hebrews may have thought they had with God because of the Law had been neutralized by Jesus Christ. In the gospel era all people were the same, according to Paul. Gentiles were on the same footing with Jews. The impartiality of God is one of the major themes of the Book of Acts.

But Paul went farther than that. He identified Jesus with the concept of Wisdom as described in the Old Testament (1 Corinthians 1:20-25). The Wisdom of God existed before the Law. If Jesus could be seen as God's Wisdom, this fact would mean that Jesus existed before the Law and therefore was its proper fulfillment. But this idea was a later development in New Testament thought. When Jesus sat on the hillside that day and taught, the idea that he himself was the fulfillment of the Law of God was a new idea. Clearly, although Jesus jolted the people, his words spoke to their hearts. At the end of the Sermon on the Mount we are told they were "astonished" at his authority (Matthew 7:28-29).

Hardly had those listeners settled down from Jesus' words about the Law when Jesus added, "For I tell you, unless your righteousness exceeds that of the scribes and Pharisees, you will never enter the kingdom of heaven" (Matthew 5:20). In today's terms that statement would be like saying we have to be more dedicated to the church than the missionary in the remotest village or the monk in the most austere monastery. Most people I know would throw up their hands and say, "No way! With our families and jobs and responsibilities, how can we possibly be more dedicated than they are? Besides, we don't have their special training." That is exactly how those who heard Jesus must have responded. Even the disciples felt this way because they were not trained professionals in religion. On the surface Jesus' demand looked hopeless. This was an impossible demand.

But Jesus was trying to get the people to think. What does God require of me? How can I live so as to show my love for God? Would God actually use me, untrained as I am, poor as I am?

It is no different now. Many Christians live a life that is spiritually dry and do not know how to get off center. In fact, you may be one of those many people who think religion is probably a good thing but does not seem to relate to the real world.

So much surface righteousness is all around us. Of

course Christianity seems shallow when all it means is attending church once or twice a week, maybe serving on a board or committee, and giving a few dollars for the programs of the church. The faith of the New Testament church was dynamic and alive.

In the Sermon on the Mount Jesus attempted to help us see that vital faith is possible when it comes from deep within. Vital faith is not a matter of keeping a set of rules, no matter how fine those rules may be. The life that comes from the good news of God is based on principles forged out of faith and lived in the power of the same Spirit who raised Jesus from the dead.

This issue is so important that Jesus gave six illustrations in the Sermon on the Mount to get his point across. Jesus did not want us to miss what he was saying; he wanted us to think! Jesus was trying to help us see that what we do, however good, does not enable us to please God and enter the Kingdom. Rather, what is in our heart, that is, the motives by which we live, is supremely important. True righteousness is more than keeping the Law. True righteousness is following faithfully Jesus as Savior and Lord. True righteousness is the life of freedom.

As we study the illustrations Jesus gave, let us not stumble over the notion of the Old Testament Law. Most of us never have lived under that kind of moral system. But all of us have lived under the expectations of moral codes, written and unwritten. The illustrations of Jesus apply to the modern world every bit as much as they did to his world.

Anger. "Every one who is angry with his brother shall be liable to judgment" (Matthew 5:22). I met a woman once who said she hated her son-in-law but loved his soul. That would be a neat trick if you could pull it off. Jesus has some advice for her and the rest of us for that matter. In Matthew 5:21-26 Jesus talked about our problem with anger. His remarks go past the letter of the Law to the heart of the matter.

The Law or any human law can only concern itself with what happens. If a wrong is done, then the Law can punish. But God looks on the heart and judges motives and feelings. The deeper way to the Kingdom means not only that we will avoid antisocial behavior but that we will allow the Spirit to cleanse us from hostile feelings.

Jesus taught that anger always kills something in the human spirit. Therefore take heed to your inner self. Mend broken relationships. Your worship of God will not be acceptable if you consciously keep resentments and anger in your heart against someone else. The deeper way is a way of peace.

Lust. "Every one who looks at a woman lustfully has already committed adultery with her in his heart" (Matthew 5:28). No system of law can haul anyone into court for thinking lustful thoughts, but what goes on in our minds is important to God. Sexual passions leading to adultery may have a variety of causes, such as a desire to dominate others, feelings of fear and anger, or uncontrolled sexual passions.

Jesus knew that meaningful social relationships and the pure worship of God flow out of the heart. A heart cluttered with frustrations cannot be at peace.

If a person entertains wrong desires and feeds those secret thoughts, then that person is no more approved by God than the person who carries out a sinful act. Jesus said our responsibility is to choose what controls our thoughts, either self-interest or love of God and neighbor. The deeper way of the Kingdom is concerned with a healthy respect for self and self-worth. It is crucial that we allow the Spirit of God to bring harmony into our lives by channeling all our energies in ways that complement the concerns of the Kingdom. Therefore, Matthew 5:27-30 helps us see how important a pure mind is to God.

Fidelity. "Every one who divorces his wife, except on the ground of unchastity, makes her an adulteress" (Matthew 5:32). Matthew 5:31-32 is related to the saying on lust and desire. Some rabbinical schools in the first century allowed a man to divorce his wife for the most trivial reasons. Married women were at the mercy of their husbands. Getting a husband who cared was important. However, if the marriage relationship soured and the marriage were dissolved, the courts tried to protect the woman's interests. The former husband was required to help support her.

While this law was helpful, Jesus was disturbed over the ease with which a man could divorce his wife. Jesus emphasized the deeper issue of fidelity in marriage. If we cannot maintain our sacred commitments to persons we can see, how can we be committed to God whom we cannot see?

Honesty. "Do not swear at all" (Matthew 5:34). In Matthew 5:33-37 Jesus reminded the people that they had been taught that, if they swear before God to do something, they had better do it! As we believe in our courts today, people then believed that greater pressure was put on persons to tell the truth if their statements were supported by oaths. People then and now assume that individuals may tend to lie or hedge the truth unless some oath is added for safekeeping. Not so, says Jesus. Simply speak the truth. If you mean yes, say so. If you mean no, say so. Following Jesus means a deep commitment to the truth.

Revenge. "Do not resist one who is evil" (Matthew 5:39). Jesus further illustrated the limited nature of the Law in Matthew 5:38-42. The Law provided that if one were unjustly harmed, that person was entitled to revenge, thus, "an eye for an eye." But Jesus said we are to resist this desire to get even. In fact, Christians are to do something extra, something kind, for the one who hurts them. All of a sudden the demands of the Kingdom seem to have taken a gigantic leap from the first illustration on anger to this one on revenge.

John Wesley strongly believed that persecuted Methodists should not take their tormentors to court for redress, even though that was their legal right. This teaching calls for great confidence in God. If this is what pleases God, this is what Christians will do. Surely their actions would show a different standard for righting wrongs.

Love of enemies. "Love your enemies and pray for those who persecute you" (Matthew 5:44). Jesus' remarks on "an eye for an eye" open the way for him to push toward this last and most demanding illustration of the deeper way. Here it is, stark and bold: *Love your enemies.* Here in Matthew 5:43-48 the word *love* surfaces for the first time in the Sermon on the Mount. Using it with reference to enemies must have caused a ripple among those who heard Jesus.

What the Lord was correcting here is a popular misconception of Old Testament Law. The Law does not teach hatred of enemies. Yet wars of retaliation and aggression were sanctioned supposedly by God's approval. But the followers of Jesus are called to love in a way that seems insane to unbelievers. Even the church, while admitting the obviously lofty ethic taught in these passages, has had difficulty agreeing on the social implications of Jesus' words.

Who are the enemies about whom Jesus spoke? In a larger sense they could be the enemies of the nation of Israel. In a narrower sense they certainly were those who violently opposed Jesus and his followers. They were people who insulted, persecuted, and falsely accused the disciples. The enemy was at times clothed in religious garb. Jesus told his disciples that the day was coming when their enemies would think they were doing God a service by persecuting them. We know Jesus himself experienced that type of national and religious hatred. But God loves God's enemies and calls on God's people to do the same. In loving under such circumstances Christians show their likeness to God. And such love is a gift of the Spirit.

Occasionally we hear someone say of another person, "She doesn't have an enemy in the world." Such a compliment is gracious but not true. We all have enemies, especially if we attempt faithfully to live according to Jesus' teachings. People may hate us enough to harm us simply because they do not like the color of our skin, our political persuasion, our nationality, or our religious convictions.

A recent student at Asbury had escaped from the terror of Idi Amin in Uganda. He told of seeing hundreds of Christians lined up and shot. The reason? Because as Christians they were considered to be a political threat. We may not know when circumstances might make martyrdom a reality.

Jesus told us to do good to the enemy. German theologian Dietrich Bonhoeffer said the enemy needs our pity. He said that no one is in deeper distress than our enemy. No service is more necessary or blessed than service to our enemies. Bonhoeffer knew what he was talking about. He spent nearly two years in a Nazi concentration camp and was finally hanged a few days before the camp was liberated.

The Christian teaching of returning good for evil is absolutely necessary if the vicious circle of violence in human relationships is to be broken. This is exactly what Jesus did, returning blessing for cursing. Christians live in the deeper way when they refuse to fight the enemy on the enemy's terms.

In the Sermon on the Plain Jesus included enemies in his words on loving others (Luke 6:27-36). There he urged his followers to *love* those who did not love them (6:32), to *do good* to them (6:33), and to *lend* to them (6:34). When we show mercy to our enemies, we behave like God (6:35-36).

In the Sermon on the Mount Jesus told us to love our enemies, which means to do good to them, bless them, and pray for them (Matthew 5:44). We imitate God's goodness when we do this.

This sounds wonderful, but who can do it? Here we seem to reach the limits of human toleration. No one can treat an enemy this way. This is clearly beyond us. We can see why this teaching has been called the impossible command. Who can command another person to love, even though that is what Jesus did? Here we seem bent on retreating into a law that provides us with the means of redress and punishment. Surely this shows how weak we are and how much we need grace and strength from God if we are even to come close to the gospel of Jesus Christ. What a dilemma! If we love the enemy, we seem to be overlooking the enemy's offenses. If we hate the enemy, we turn our backs on the gospel.

At this point we need to remember the authority

with which Jesus gave these six illustrations. Jesus did not appeal to the opinions of learned teachers or provide footnotes for documentation to validate his views. He simply said, "I say to you" (Matthew 5:22, 28, 32, 34, 39, 44). His hearers could not miss the force of these words. And this point is crucial for us. Jesus is either Lord—one who has absolute authority over us—or he is not. It is a matter of choosing, taking sides, a matter of being committed to his way or going in another direction.

Here is the gospel, the good news. God gave Jesus Christ for us. Herein lies the strength we need to do what God expects of us. God suffers with us to bring about God's purposes. Jesus died, forgiving those who brutally murdered him. Here is our model—Jesus himself. God has sent the Holy Spirit to help us do what otherwise would be impossible for us.

With our hearts hidden in God we can love and forgive and restore the most wretched person imaginable. We need Christ's help because we experience terrible pressure to hate. Following Christ, we risk being called cowards by our enemies and traitors by our friends. Yet we follow him and beg for strength to live like him.

Obviously the deeper way requires discipline of soul. The deeper way requires that we know ourselves with all our limitations and fears and that we not deceive ourselves by thinking we are strong when we are actually weak. The deeper way requires that we develop a spirit of humility, obedience, and prayer. Humility can keep us from falling away. Obedience enables us to follow Jesus regardless of the personal cost. Prayer helps us keep all our experiences in proper relationship with one another. We must learn to rely on God and not on ourselves.

To grow in love the way Jesus teaches, we must value him above all else. We must listen to him for his personal word for our lives. When we think the way is impossible, then we go to our knees to confess our sin of unbelief and to praise God's goodness and patience with us. The Holy Spirit will come to our aid if we ask.

3

A Secret Way

The royal way is a secret way. In Matthew 6:1-18 Jesus talked about private piety. He said that God sees what we do in secret. God knows not only our actions but our intentions.

Writing to the Philippians Paul said, "Do nothing from selfishness or conceit, but in humility count others better than yourselves" (Philippians 2:3). How far from our actual practice are the words, "count others better than yourselves"? So that we could not possibly miss what he was saying, Paul continued, "Have this mind among yourselves, which is yours in Christ Jesus, who, though he was in the form of God, did not count equality with God a thing to be grasped, but emptied himself, taking the form of a servant, being born in the likeness of men. And being found in human form he humbled himself and became obedient unto death, even death on a cross" (Philippians 2:5-8).

This ancient hymn to Christ deserves a prominent place in our meditations. Note the words: "emptied himself," "form of a servant," "humbled himself," and "became obedient unto death." Was there ever a better, more fitting summary of the life of Jesus Christ? He who was the Word made flesh, he who now lives on high, he who is Lord of the church through his Spirit—this same Jesus lived a life of self-giving and genuine humility. All of us who compare our lives with Jesus find we are miserably lacking in these two virtues. Without regard to our distance from him, Jesus still draws us to himself and goes about making us into his holy people.

Humility has been defined as a virtue derived from a profound sense of reverence toward God. Virtue lies in recognizing our true position with respect to our Creator and fellow creatures and in shaping our conduct in accordance with that position.

Reverence for God and worship of God show us what we are—self-serving sinners. That insight produces humility, because we realize we have no goodness of our own to claim. Our true position in relation to God is that of a beggar. The definition also means that we are no better than the next person. All of us are on the same level. Therefore, we live daily by the biblical ideas that we share a common humanity with all people and that we receive mercy from God. Having nothing to brag about in ourselves, we brag on the Lord!

Of course, some people do not like that notion of humility. Some say, "Don't think of yourself as a worm! Stand up and be counted!" At times this may be good advice, but it may lead us away from genuine humility.

A humble spirit is not simply a "poor me" attitude. It is not thinking of yourself as a worm. Far from it! A humble spirit is not thinking "How disgusting I am" or "How undeserving I am." The classical spiritual writers tell us that humble persons, self-denying persons, simply do not think of themselves at all; they think of God. Put another way, Christians should be more concerned about God's glory than about their own rights.

God seems to delight in using quite ordinary people to accomplish God's will. God chose Israel, a small and insignificant group of people, to take God's message to the Promised Land. Jesus came from the home of a carpenter. He had no special privileges, no social status, and no political clout. Over and over God has used the powerless and pitiful people of the world to do God's will. As a result, the Christian church never has put much stock in giving awards or special recognitions. Our worth is derived from Christ and is nurtured in the secret life of good works, fasting, and prayer.

The Scripture passage for this chapter combats a serious threat to vital Christian experience. That threat is pride. The problem with pride is that it provides a false sense of confidence and worth. The proud person thinks herself or himself a cut above the ordinary individual. The recognition and acclaim that our society gives certain people seem to indicate that those people are more talented, more beautiful, more popular, or more generous—somehow worth more—than other people. Only a few individuals can be on top in the eyes of our society.

But in the eyes of Jesus everyone is on top! Jesus deflates the proud and inflates the poor and in doing so brings a common dignity to all of us.

The writer of the First Letter of John warned, "Do not love the world or the things in the world. If any one loves the world, love for the Father is not in him. For all that is in the world, the lust of the flesh and the lust of the eyes and the pride of life, is not of the Father but is of the world" (1 John 2:15-16). The idea here of "the pride of life" suggests boasting of what one has and does and is translated that way in the New International Version of the Bible.

If we do not hunger and thirst for God, we will hunger and thirst for advantage, power, and status. The *proud* are variously pictured in Scripture as being arrogant, insolent, presumptuous, haughty, and given to boasting prattle. Jesus warned us against such attitudes in this section of the Sermon on the Mount.

The first of Jesus' teachings in this section of the Sermon on the Mount has to do with charitable deeds. Jesus seemed to expect that those who have an abundance of worldly goods will share their excess with people who have needs. It is important that we see ourselves as responsible for the needs of others. It is also important *how* we share and what attitude we have when we give to others.

Jesus told the people that, when they did good works, they should follow the old proverb, "Do not let your left hand know what your right hand is doing" (Matthew 6:3). In other words, don't make a big show of being kind to the down-and-out. People who do this are hypocrites, Jesus said. They are not actually helping others so much as they are trying to buy applause.

A hypocrite is someone who puts up a false front. The word comes from the ancient Greek actor who wore a mask to depict his mood. The "mask wearers" Jesus talked about were those very rich persons who had their presence in the square announced by the blowing of trumpets. The surface reason for doing this was to let the beggars know a benefactor had arrived to help them. But Jesus knew the hidden reason was to give the patron publicity so he could be admired for what he was doing.

No doubt many people were helped by money given for this selfish reason. The giver's hypocrisy probably did not matter at all to the poor person who received the gift. But it did matter to Jesus, because Jesus saw the rich using the poor, not having compassion on them, not giving out of love. The rich were enhancing their own status at the expense of the poor.

When I say "at the expense of the poor," I mean these hypocrites gained prestige by crushing the last ounce of dignity the poor had left. The basis for social standing was pretty much the same then as now.

Important then and important now are how much money you have, what your family background is, and how much political pull you have. Having someone below you on the social ladder, someone you could look down on, determined social status for first-century people as it does for us. This way you always look good by comparison. Thus when we give to help meet the needs of the poor in a condescending manner, we show ourselves to be hypocrites in the eyes of God.

Jesus identified with those on the very bottom of the social scale. For Jesus these social castoffs were made in the image of God, just as were the rich. On the basis of a common humanity and the need for compassion for its weaker members, Jesus condemned the generous hypocrites for making a public spectacle of the poor so their own lust for recognition could be satisfied.

Jesus' teaching here emphasizes the Jewish idea of charity (giving in love). According to the oral law, the lowest level of charity, least pleasing to God, was giving directly to one in need. The highest level of charity, most pleasing to God, was giving without knowing who would receive the gift. Jesus here criticized those who had missed the mark and gave for their own selfish purposes.

Jesus was born a friend of the poor. The Gospel of Luke reports that when Mary visited her kinswoman Elizabeth before Jesus was born, she broke into song, praising God for what God was doing for God's people. Part of her song includes the following statement:

"He has put down the mighty from their thrones,
and has exalted those of low degree;
he has filled the hungry with good things,
and the rich he has sent empty away" (Luke 1:52-53).

Years later Jesus went to the synagogue in his home town of Nazareth. Asked to read from the scroll, the Lord picked up Isaiah's prophecy. Unrolling the scroll, he read:

"The Spirit of the Lord is upon me,
because he has anointed me to preach good news to
  the poor.
He has sent me to proclaim release to the captives
and recovering of sight to the blind,
to set at liberty those who are oppressed,
to proclaim the acceptable year of the Lord" (Luke
  4:18-19).

Though these two texts from Luke refer mainly to the nation, they have powerful meaning for the poor. Jesus went first to the poor, the lame, the maimed, the lepers, and the outcasts. Jesus shocked the sophisticated people of his time by eating with "sinners" (Matthew 9:10-11), and sometimes he did not even wash his hands first (Luke 11:37-38). Jesus openly forgave the greed of the tax collectors and the lusts and hates of the sexually promiscuous. Jesus had a reputation in some circles for eating too much and drinking too much wine (Matthew 11:19). Jesus identified with the diseased and the different. "Those who are well have no need of a physician," Jesus said, "but those who are sick" (Matthew 9:12). It was to the "lost sheep" of Israel that he went first. When he deemed it necessary, Jesus broke sabbath laws (Matthew 12:1-8, 9-13). To make matters worse he occasionally made heroes of the Samaritans, seemed to ignore the problems of the Roman occupation, and called the religious leaders "hypocrites" and "blind guides" (Matthew 23:13-36).

Hudson Taylor, founder of the China Inland Mission, one of the largest mission efforts in China, understood what Jesus meant. Taylor knew that to get a hearing he had to stop being English and become Chinese. By the time he reached middle age he spoke, looked, and dressed so much like a Mandarin Chinese man that he was accepted everywhere he went as the real thing. And by that time he was. Taylor did not go to China to stoop down to the common laborers with a gospel handout. Rather, he identified with them so he could help lift them up. Taylor gave respect and dignity to the Chinese people he met. This is exactly what Jesus did. And this is what we will do for the outcasts of society if we really follow Jesus.

It is one thing to read about what Jesus did day in and day out without fanfare or publicity stunts. It is quite another for those of us who say we love him to go out in his name and do the same thing. We are to lose ourselves in our gifts, not seeking or accepting notoriety or acclaim. Only then are we free to give and give. The God who sees our secret works will reward us in God's own time. For now, the privilege of serving the poor is enough.

"When you pray, go into your room and shut the door and pray to your Father who is in secret" (Matthew 6:6). Prayer is sacred. It is communion with God. Go to God in secret, Jesus said. Enter your room. Pray apart. This idea of praying in secret is important for the whole of our devotional lives. We are shaped and polished to be the vessels of God in the private place of prayer. Some people do not witness to their faith simply because they have none. But some find witnessing difficult because they cannot express the deep inner relationship they have with God. Intimate matters are difficult to talk about, and this is true in our relationship with God.

Jesus warned us about the ways of another hypocrite, the one who prays without really praying. In Jesus' time this was the person who would go to public places and at the time for prayer make a show of supposed piety. Actually people like this want others to see them and say, "My, isn't that person spiritual?" But God does not hear prayers addressed to humans. Jesus said that we are to pray in secret and God will give us God's blessing.

Of course, at times public prayer is expected, such as in worship services, small group meetings, or with a friend. But Jesus had a caution for that too. Do not waste your time praying with elaborate, flowery language. Do not repeat meaningless phrases. God is not impressed with those prayers. Someone who sees or hears us may think we are quite religious, but God is not fooled.

Prayer is so important, so private, that Jesus suggested a way to pray. We call this model prayer the Lord's Prayer, and the Gospels give us two versions:

"Our Father who art in heaven,
Hallowed be thy name.
Thy kingdom come,
Thy will be done,
  On earth as it is in heaven.
Give us this day our daily bread;
And forgive us our debts,
  As we also have forgiven our debtors;
And lead us not into temptation,
  But deliver us from evil" (Matthew 6:9-13).

"Father, hallowed be thy name. Thy kingdom come. Give us each day our daily bread; and forgive us our sins, for we ourselves forgive every one who is indebted to us; and lead us not into temptation" (Luke 11:2-4).

Prayer is so important for growth in God's love that it must be cultivated in private. In prayer we come to know ourselves. We see how our true identity and our deep needs are intertwined. We also come to know God as loving and responding.

All of our life is or should be a prayer. All life is listening to God and responding to what we hear. Prayer is asking and adoration. It is time spent, unrushed, in God's presence.

Jesus Christ maintained that we are forgiven by God only if we forgive others. A heart filled with bitterness toward another person cannot at the same time be filled with praise to God. Our human life and our relationships are directly connected with our prayer to God. Any part of life that is violated by hatred or envy is a hindrance to prayer and holiness. Jesus helps us see that a heart filled with God forgives automatically, for God is love (1 John 4:8).

Jesus' last illustration on the secret life of the kingdom revolves around fasting. "When you fast, anoint your head and wash your face, that your fasting may not be seen by men" (Matthew 6:17-18). Jesus was saying, in effect, "Don't make it obvious so others will notice." Many times we like for others to know what trials we are going through, even self-imposed ones, so we can feed off their admiration. I think Jesus' remarks are a warning against parading our acts of self-denial in front of others.

At first this instruction seems like such a little thing. But this really strikes at the root of spirituality. Since spiritual life is the gift of God, we need to reserve parts of our lives and experiences for God alone. Fasting indicates a sincere heart in search of God. To let others in on what we are doing may cancel out what we had hoped for in the first place—communion with God.

Fasting has positive benefits when done in the right spirit. We must never see fasting as a sort of arm-twisting, a manipulation of God to get what we want. Fasting is one form of self-denial that can draw us deeper into the life of pure faith.

First, if we deny ourselves food for a while, we can better pray for the hungry of the world. The spiritual principle here is that shared pain produces compassion and the true spirit of intercession.

Second, fasting and prayer become love gifts to God when we take time that is usually ours and give it back to God in adoration and praise.

Third, some acts of ministry require a special kind of spiritual power that can come only from prayer and fasting.

By now we see Jesus' message on the importance of the inner life. We also see that it is important for us to be alone with God and to do some of our spiritual disciplines for God alone. We also see that such acts of righteousness done in secret show us that public acclaim of our works is not necessary for them to be effective. Of course, we also discover that the humility so characteristic of Jesus comes from good works, prayer, and fasting, all done without seeking crowd approval.

All of us need a private place for prayer and meditation. And our secret life of prayer, praise, and work for the Kingdom provides the stability, power, and love we need for the public side of our ministry.

4

A Restful Way

The royal way is a restful way. In Matthew 6:19-34 and Luke 6:20-26 Jesus described a life of simplicity and peace.

Jesus Christ calls us to follow him in the way of abounding joy, increasingly deeper manifestations of God's grace in our hearts, and constant secret devotion and humility.

Already we have seen some of the wonderful benefits of following Jesus Christ as Savior and Lord—a sense of sins forgiven, the establishment of a relationship with God, life lived with a sense of purpose and destiny, and the cultivation of those virtues that bring out the best in us and also enhance the lives of those we touch.

These blessings come to those whose lives are centered on Christ. Everything else in life finds its place and meaning in relation to Jesus Christ. Our ancestors were called "Christians" first at Antioch because of their sincere attempts to imitate Christ's life.

This life of simplicity and peace that Christ calls us to lead is the kind of life that trusts God for daily needs. Confidence in God leads us into a life of calm and peace, free from anxiety.

Jesus said, "Do not lay up for yourselves treasures on earth, where moth and rust consume and where thieves break in and steal, but lay up for yourselves treasures in heaven, where neither moth nor rust consumes and where thieves do not break in and steal. For where your treasure is, there will your heart be also" (Matthew 6:19-21).

Jesus' sayings in the Scripture passages for this chapter relate to the way we use money and other valuables. So this chapter may be controversial. It may tell us some things we do not want to hear.

Money is a thorn in our side. We never seem to have enough of it regardless of how much we have. We constantly have to decide what to do with our money, whether we have a little or a lot. The poor want money, and the rich want more money. Money and other things of value have an unbelievable attraction for us. Because so much of our time and interest is devoted to making money, money is of special concern to Christians.

Few things threaten vital spirituality more than the rampant materialism of our day. The mad scramble in our society for wealth and status at times invades the church and ruins lives. At the same time we need the security and leisure that money provides if we are to develop wholesome relationships with our families and friends. The use of money is at best a thorny problem.

Christians are to be concerned with the proper use of money but not overly concerned with accumulating money. Seeking this balance creates special tensions for the church when the church exists in a society in which money and status are highly valued as ends in themselves. Christians unwittingly contribute to this type of mindset when we counsel our children to go into certain lines of work because of the amount of money they will make and the material benefits they will receive.

Three general benefits of wealth are power, possessions, and prestige. All three run counter to the plain teachings of Jesus in the Scripture passages we are studying in this chapter. The people of the first century were every bit as much captivated by these benefits of money as we are today. But Jesus told his disciples (and us) that it is not wise to spend time stockpiling valuables on earth.

Although Jesus addresses our contemporary problems with money, the word *treasure* can be applied to anything we depend on for personal identity and meaning in life. In a real sense, health, career, family, and other things are equally as important as money in what they seem to do for us. The sayings of Jesus related to money can be used to understand our relationship to whatever seems to be the center of our lives.

John Wesley was concerned with the use of money. Reflecting on the notion of "treasures," Wesley defined treasures as goods and money *in excess* of what is needed to pay the bills of the household, purchase modest clothing and food, set aside a modest amount as insurance against death, and provide enough reserve money to help keep one's business solvent.

We must remember that when Wesley used words like *modest* to describe the Christian lifestyle, that is exactly what he meant. He expected Methodists to be industrious, frugal, and sharing. Recall his famous advice to earn all you can, save all you can, and give all you can. I believe Wesley and Jesus agree on what constitutes treasure.

Some monastic orders and some Protestants interpret Jesus' words to mean that we should literally give our treasures away and follow Christ. In this way Christians would be totally dependent on God. But unless one is called to a vow of poverty, some saving and investing may be necessary to provide for a family. I also think that John Wesley was right in suggesting that giving to the support of one's family is in fact giving to God. Wesley warned us, however, that hoarding goods or money is robbing from the poor.

Wesley's notion that an excessive stockpiling of goods is robbing the poor is strong language. But Wesley was right. One reason why Christians must give serious attention to their understanding of wealth is that accumulating wealth creates an imbalance in the distribution of goods. This imbalance is bad enough on the surface, but it seems even more sinful when we take seriously the biblical teaching that all the people of the earth are essentially one family. Simply stated, we are one another's keepers. We are to care especially for the person who is in no condition to care for himself or herself. Whether the person in need is a Christian is not supposed to be a concern.

A second problem with overvaluing wealth is that the time and energy that people spend in getting wealthy is disproportionate to what wealth can actually do for a person. We know from the tragedies in the lives of the wealthy that material prosperity does not prevent family problems, personal emotional disorder, or violent behavior. Jesus' words about the possibility of losing wealth (Matthew 6:19) are a great warning to those persons who think that wealth itself can bring happiness.

A third consideration about treasures is that the pursuit of wealth tends to create a spirit of competition between people that is flagrantly unchristian. Competition in sports is one thing; unbridled competition in business is another. Christians are forbidden by Christ's teachings on love to speak evil of a competitor or to try and drive that competitor out of business. The desire for wealth tends to breed competition between people rather than compassion for people.

A fourth reason why we Christians must rethink our view of wealth is that wealth can threaten our relationship with God. Jesus talked of having two bosses: "No one can serve two masters" (Matthew

6:24). Sooner or later we will have to choose between them, between riches and God. One implication of Jesus' saying is that even Christians will be tempted to choose short-run gratification rather than long-run spiritual relationship. Greed and the fear of insecurity are always lurking in the minds of people, even Christians.

Finally, if Christ is really our Lord, then we are to follow his teaching. When Jesus told people to give up their possessions before they could follow him, he was doing more than humbling the proud. Jesus' disciples went out sharing the good news of redemption. The good news, of course, involves human social life as well as human personal redemption. The good news is that a loving God is calling people away from their illusions about happiness, away from their false supports and toward a radical dependence on God's salvation. When Christians share what they have with others, they are living examples of the power of the gospel to change lives for the better.

Jesus' ministry was primarily concerned with the poor. Although we already have touched on what the Sermon on the Mount says about the poor, we cannot properly understand the Scripture for this chapter without discussing the poor again. The Gospels were written originally for a church under persecution, a church whose membership was largely poor economically.

The Methodists began as a poorer class movement in England. Not until the middle of the nineteenth century in America could the Methodist movement be considered middle class. The upward mobility we have experienced from that time until now has been due largely to our strict adherence to the Protestant work ethic—an honest day's work and an honest day's wage. We must be careful in our affluence that we do not distort the teachings of Jesus or lose touch with our beginnings.

As the first beatitude in Matthew shows us, the inhabitants of the Kingdom of heaven are poor spiritually. That is, Jesus came first to the house of

Israel, and within that house he came first to the literal poor.

With this background in mind, consider the blessings and woes found in Luke's Sermon on the Plain:

"Blessed are you poor, for yours is the kingdom of God.

"Blessed are you that hunger now, for you shall be satisfied.

"Blessed are you that weep now, for you shall laugh.

"Blessed are you when men hate you, and when they exclude you and revile you, and cast out your name as evil, on account of the Son of man! Rejoice in that day, and leap for joy, for behold, your reward is great in heaven; for so their fathers did to the prophets.

"But woe to you that are rich, for you have received your consolation.

"Woe to you that are full now, for you shall hunger.

"Woe to you that laugh now, for you shall mourn and weep.

"Woe to you, when all men speak well of you, for so their fathers did to the false prophets" (Luke 6:20-26).

Poverty is a broad term and actually means more than being penniless or hungry. Widows in biblical times were considered poor because they were helpless. The lame, the blind, the insane were considered poor because they were defenseless. Poverty is a denial of the goodness of God. It is a blight on the biblical truth that all people are made in the divine image. One reason why the poor serve as a good analogy for spiritual life is that they tend to be meek because they lack the ability and power to take up their own cause. A common message of both testaments is that God loves the poor, and the people of God are expected to come to the aid of those in poverty.

The problem of poverty is compounded today because multiplied millions of people have been reduced to the lowest and most debased level of human life. If people are to take our gospel seriously, they must see evidence of its power among the weaker peoples of the world. But relieving the plight of the poor is still not a popular idea. Our churches reflect this reluctance. Most of our recent church growth has been in the suburbs and small towns near cities. The number of ministers called to inner city ministries or other work among the poor is quite small. Most of the church's ministry is to the comfortable people, far from the misery and squalor of basic human need.

Loving wealth without having much of it is possible. This happens every time we gamble our earnings in order to strike it rich. It happens when we spend more on ourselves than necessity demands. It happens when we have a closet full of clothes and moan that we do not have anything to wear. It happens when we buy expensive luxury items in an attempt to impress someone else. It happens when we give to charity in ways that call attention to us or to our gift. It happens whenever we fall for slick advertising that promises us power and status as a result of using a certain product.

This is why Christians must choose. Will our boss, our master, the controlling interest of our life be God's will? Or will it be the pull of earthly valuables? These two value systems cannot exist side by side in our hearts. Both demand time, energy, and devotion. Only one can reign supreme. The only question Jesus poses for us is which one will be the master. By setting the love of God and the pursuit of wealth at opposite ends, Jesus sets the stage for a stark decision. It is not an easy decision, but it is a necessary decision for Christians.

Jesus said our eyes are like lamps for the body (Matthew 6:22). If our eyes are "sound," that is, if we see clearly, the whole body will be filled with light. But if darkness prevails, we will most certainly be deceived. In this context, Jesus is saying that trust in God is light and that trust in valuables is darkness. If our light—what is most important to us—is the mad chase after earthly valuables, then we live in great darkness. In the spirit of the first of the Ten Commandments, laying up valuables on earth is a form of idolatry.

The valuables of the kingdom of God have been set forth in the Beatitudes. These are the treasures we are to seek with all our hearts.

Always remember you are a sinner saved by God's grace. Therefore, value *humility*.

Always seek God's forgiveness and mercy. Therefore, value *repentance*.

Always fully trust God's way of doing things. Therefore, value *dependence* on God.

Always yearn for an upright life. Therefore, value *obedience*.

Always interact with others on the principle of love. Therefore, value *compassion*.

Always want a pure love for God. Therefore, value *simplicity*.

Always seek healing for broken relationships. Therefore, value *peace*.

Always return good for evil. Therefore, value *endurance*.

This is the way of perfect rest, the way of the kingdom of God. The two ways Jesus presents for us are opposed to each other. In summary we see that God's way is a way of total giving, genuine compassion, self-denial, obedience to the Holy Spirit, and meekness. Wealth's way is a way of selfish getting, unfair competition, self-indulgence, obedience to the power structures, and aggression.

Jesus calls us to trust God's love. We are more important than birds or weeds (Matthew 6:26, 30). If God cares for them, how much more will God care for us? One difference between Christians and people of the world is that we do not run frantically even after necessities. We work hard and trust God's providence.

Jesus never encouraged laziness. So Christians have been hard and often creative workers. The tone for discipleship was set by the apostle Paul. Even though he was entitled to be supported by the churches because of his traveling ministry, he rarely accepted gifts from churches. As a skilled tentmaker, Paul was able to earn his own living and meet his own needs except when in prison. He was so convinced Christians should provide for themselves that Paul said if a person does not work that person should not eat (2 Thessalonians 3:10). In addition, Paul taught that the Christian who does not provide for the needs of his own family is worse than a rank unbeliever (1 Timothy 5:8). Finally, Paul said Christians should protect the dignity of the poor and disabled by sharing with them.

So the final word for this chapter is trust God in heaven. Seek God's kingdom. Put your energy into serving God. God provides us with the necessities. How does God do this? First, by providing us with honest work. Second, by equipping us with basic skills and the mental ability to work. Third, God gives us the church, which will nurture us and help us in times of need. Therefore, live moderate lives, trust God completely, seek God's kingdom, and share what you have with those who need it. Do these things from a grateful heart, and you will be at rest as God's dear children.

5

A Humble Way

The royal way is a humble way. In Matthew 7:1-12 and Luke 6:37-45 Jesus described the life of humility and dependence on God.

The Sermon on the Mount opened with the beatitude, "Blessed are the poor in spirit, for theirs is the kingdom of heaven" (Matthew 5:3). We have seen that this teaching is basic to vital life in Christ. The deep sense of one's need for God is the beginning point of the humble life. As we grow in Christ, this virtue, this humility, grows. True humility is born in the human heart that seeks God alone. The truly humble person is the person who has learned that God is all.

Recently I heard a young woman describe her relationship to God in the following way. "I recently married," she said. "I didn't realize that my love for my husband might conflict with my love for God. I had to come quickly to the place where I was married in my devotion to my husband but still single in my devotion to God."

This young woman spoke with deep spiritual insight. She realized that as much as she loved her husband, she could not allow her love for him to overshadow her love for God. She spoke in the spirit of the first beatitude. She realized that a humble life of dependency on God must determine her priorities. This insight will prove to be a great blessing for her. She will also learn that the deeper one grows in faith the more one senses the need of divine grace. That knowledge alone will help keep this young woman in true humility.

Two other beatitudes are also important to the life of humility. They are the ones on meekness and mercy. "Blessed are the meek, for they shall inherit the earth" (Matthew 5:5). "Blessed are the merciful, for they shall obtain mercy" (Matthew 5:7). The prophet Micah told the people what true religion was when he said:

"He has showed you, O man, what is good;
and what does the LORD require of you
but to do justice, and to love kindness,
and to walk humbly with your God?" (Micah 6:8).

For the purposes of this chapter we will yoke these two beatitudes—humility and mercy—together. Our meekness or humility is expressed primarily before God and our mercy expressed toward others. These two beatitudes are like the twin commandments of Jesus: Love God with all you are, and love your neighbor as your very own self. And our Lord said that *all* the Law and the prophets were summed up in those two commandments (Matthew 22:37-40).

When humility and mercy are not cultivated, problems crop up like the one in our Scripture readings. The particular problem here is faultfinding. A judgmental spirit cancels out true humility because it assumes the right to speak in a harsh, critical way about someone else. And speaking judgmentally about someone cancels out mercy, because the judgmental person has no real concern about the feelings and welfare of the one being judged. According to

Jesus, a judgmental spirit is self-righteous and censorious. It is being the wolf rather than the lamb.

God's people must continually be on guard against the tendency to judge. Being a Christian is much more than joining the church or even praying and reading the Bible. To be a Christian is to be committed to the spirit of Jesus. This commitment shows in the desire to be like Jesus as much as possible. Our commitment to the spirit of Jesus is seen in how we treat other people when we display kindness, mercy, and love.

The sign of our intentions to love Christ and follow him is our baptism.

In the early church new converts were normally baptized on Easter Sunday morning as a sign of their death to the world and their new life in Christ. The *catechumens* (the ones who had been taught the Christian way and were about to join the church) faced the outside of the building as they publicly renounced their former lives and the evils of the world. Then, turning to face the minister, they affirmed their new faith in Jesus Christ as their Savior and Lord. In this way of renunciation and affirmation, the new converts visibly symbolized that they had counted the cost of discipleship and were willing to pay the price.

Christians face trials and temptations from without and from within. The temptations of Jesus (Matthew 4:1-11) are examples of the kinds of pressures we face. Like Jesus we are tempted to seek prestige, power, and popularity. To combat what Paul called evil "principalities and powers," we need at least four qualities. These are humility, the greatest vigilance, the will to resist, and prayer.

As we can easily see, all of these four graces relate to the beatitudes on humility and mercy. When lived out, the characteristics of Christian awareness bring honor to the gospel. And the heart of the gospel is the knowledge that God was revealed to be both humble and merciful when God was revealed in Jesus.

In the four graces listed above, humility is the first requirement for victory over evil. The opposite of humility is pride. Both Old and New Testaments agree that pride blinds us. Only humility restores our sight and lets us see the mind of God.

The second grace is having the greatest vigilance. This means that we are to be on the lookout lest we be blinded by evil influences. To be vigilant in faith is to be serious about faith. As we caution our children to be careful, so we too must be careful not to bring dishonor on the Lord.

The third grace is having a will to resist. That is having the ability and the determination to say no to evil influences. If we set our will to follow Christ, then we will not fail to inherit the Kingdom.

Finally, the fourth grace is prayer, a subject we already have considered. Prayer makes us strong in faith and helps us to grow in humility and mercy.

In your prayers at the beginning of the day, remember these four graces and ask God to increase them in your life each day. Again, these graces are constant humility, constant watchfulness against evil, constant willingness to resist evil, and constant prayer to God for aid.

"Judge not, that you be not judged. For with the judgment you pronounce you will be judged, and the measure you give will be the measure you get. Why do you see the speck that is in your brother's eye, but do not notice the log that is in your own eye?" (Matthew 7:1-3).

Jesus once told a story that helps us understand his remarks about the "log" and the "speck" in the eye. It seems that two men went to the Temple to pray. One was a Pharisee, a religious traditionalist and strict observer of the Law. The other was a tax collector, a social outcast in the eyes of the Jews. The Pharisee stood up straight and prayed to God, "God, I thank thee that I am not like other men, extortioners, unjust, adulterers, or even like this tax collector. I fast twice a week, I give tithes of all that I get" (Luke 18:11-12).

The Scripture says that the tax collector stood back, not counting himself worthy to approach the altar area. It was common for people to stand at prayer with their heads lifted toward heaven. But the tax collector would not look up. Rather, he beat his chest as a sign of remorse and accusation and cried out, "God, be merciful to me a sinner!" (Luke 18:13). After telling this story Jesus said, "I tell you, this man went down to his house justified rather than the other" (Luke 18:14). And Jesus explained why: "Every one who exalts himself will be humbled, but he who humbles himself will be exalted" (Luke 18:14).

As we reflect on this parable, we notice that the Pharisee had at least two problems. First, he had a false assumption about the tax collector. He put the tax collector in the same company with the most despicable people, outright sinners like unrepentant thieves and lustful people. The Pharisee allowed general public opinion to determine how he would view the tax collector. He did not show the least concern that the tax collector had come to pray and to seek God. He judged the tax collector without knowing anything about him as a person. His own self-righteousness was the basis of his judgment of the other person.

The Pharisee's second problem was his false assumptions about himself. Because of his rigid keeping of the Law and his being known as an orthodox Jew, he assumed he was in right standing with God. It is true that other people would have considered him a righteous man. But his legalism had closed his mind to his own prejudice and arrogance. He did not go away from prayer justified before God! He went away clothed only in the righteousness of his own works. The Pharisee did not realize that he had no spiritual power. He lived in delusion. He was in every sense of the term a man with a "log" in his eye.

The log-in-the-eye syndrome shows immediately that three things are missing in a person who judges others.

First, patience is missing. In Matthew 7:1-5 we find a person who sees a little fault in someone else and hurries out to correct the situation. The first thing the judgmental person needed was to wait and consider his or her own attitude.

49

Second, compassion is missing. The spirit of the judgmental person is sharp, and the mood is impersonal. The self-righteous person does not identify with the sinner. Even the holiest person is subject to grave temptation. Jesus showed us by his life that tender compassion is necessary whenever we are dealing with the spiritual problems of others.

Third, self-understanding is missing. The "log" person has a hard heart. The judgmental person always overrates herself or himself.

Of course, the "log" person was partially right. The "speck" person had an honest-to-goodness problem. The tax collector's problem seemed obvious to the Pharisee. The tax collector was a renegade who taxed his own people for personal profit and on behalf of the Romans. We do not know what the tax collector thought his problem was, but that is not important. He called himself "a sinner."

Our judgment on people outside the church is sinful enough, but how often do we act as self-righteous judges on those within the church? those at worship? those at prayer? This is detestable in God's sight. It is hypocritical for one seeker to say or imply that another seeker is unspiritual or unacceptable to God. Yet this happens all the time. Even a true accusation, rendered in the spirit of this Scripture, cancels the accuser's own right standing before God and suddenly drops that person from the heights to a position lower than that of conspicuous sinners.

Avoiding this spirit of criticism is difficult, for it is all around us. But we can rise above the pervasive spirit of criticism. Here is an example. Two monks were talking one day with the respected elder, Abbot Poemen. One of the brothers complimented the other by saying, "He is a good brother; he hates evil." The old abbot asked, "What do you mean, he hates evil?" The brother was confused and did not know what to say. He finally asked the abbot, "Father, what is it to hate evil?" The wise abbot responded, "That man hates evil who hates his own sins, and looks upon every brother as a saint and loves him as a saint."

Here is tremendous insight. Christians should spend more time accusing themselves and praising others. If they do that, they cannot judge others wrongly. And it really does not matter whether this passage refers to our relationships with believers or nonbelievers. We already have heard that we are to love our enemies. Think of God, not of the sins of others.

If we must correct someone else, then we must do so with much caution and prayer, always considering ourselves less worthy than the one we are correcting. "I can't help it," someone might say. "A criticism comes to mind, and I say it before I know it." If that is the case, then we must be like the desert monk who carried a rock in his mouth for three years to cure himself of talking too much.

Luke's Sermon on the Plain highlights the need for wisdom in the way we talk about other people. "Judge not, and you will not be judged; condemn not, and you will not be condemned; forgive, and you will be forgiven" (Luke 6:37).

Jesus warned us not to judge or condemn but to forgive and to share. We will be treated by God the same way we treat others. As Jesus said, if we give to others God will give back to us "good measure, pressed down, shaken together, running over" (Luke 6:38). That is, we will receive a full blessing from God, more than we could reasonably expect.

Jesus told his disciples that a pupil is not above the teacher (Luke 6:40). This means that his disciples could not set their own standards of behavior. Rather, disciples are to imitate their teacher and Lord by being forgiving and loving, especially toward those who deserve it least. If they do this, they will be leaders who can see clearly and they will be able to lead others to the safety of the Kingdom. But if disciples attempt to establish their own righteousness and are harsh toward others, then they will be like a blind man trying to lead other blind men. All of them fall into ruin (Luke 6:39).

Using another analogy, Jesus said judgmental

51

people are like bad trees that produce bad fruit (Luke 6:43-45). In other words, harsh judgment comes from a heart dominated by evil and self-righteousness. Only blessings come from the heart of the person who is truly righteous.

Jesus expected his followers to exercise wisdom in their treatment of others. Jesus recognized that some people delight in mocking sacred things and hurting the followers of Christ. We disciples will have enemies, as Jesus did. At his own trial Jesus set an example of the caution we are to have toward those who are brimming over with hatred for Christ's way. He let his accusers condemn themselves.

"Do not give dogs what is holy; and do not throw your pearls before swine," Jesus said (Matthew 7:6). Dogs and swine were considered unclean by Jews. Our Lord here said that even though we would like to share our faith with all people freely, sometimes we cannot do it. This is very important. The same Jesus who earlier said we are not to judge people rashly here said that we are to be discriminating when we encounter brutality and shameless behavior. We must have great wisdom. Some people we treat with deference; others we treat with caution. In neither case, however, are we permitted to speak judgmentally and with an unkind spirit.

How are we to get the wisdom we need to live truly humble lives? Jesus said we should learn to pray (Matthew 7:7). We are to pray to God who gives wisdom. If we pray for such discernment, God will give it to us. A prayer for insight will be answered. If we ask, we will get what we need. If we seek, we will find God's will. If we knock, the door of insight and love will be opened to us.

And God is eager to help us, desiring that we receive God's good gifts. If an earthly parent delights in giving his or her children good gifts, how much more will God delight in giving good gifts to those who ask (Matthew 7:9-11)?

Though it is not common knowledge among us, the humble tax collector who was ridiculed by the

Pharisee played a significant part in Eastern Christian spirituality. The tax collector's prayer, "God, be merciful to me a sinner" (Luke 18:13), has been joined with the plea of the two blind men in Matthew 9:27, "Have mercy on us, Son of David" to make what is now called "the Jesus prayer." This simple prayer, "Lord Jesus Christ, Son of God, have mercy on me a sinner," is a prayer of contrition and humility. The Jesus prayer has been a means of blessing for many Christians who repeat it often, in part or whole. Many people use this prayer at the beginning of a period of meditation.

This section of Jesus' teachings ends with the famous Golden Rule: "So whatever you wish that men would do to you, do so to them" (Matthew 7:12).

Many religious teachers have spoken words of advice like these. But Jesus stated the rule positively, emphasizing grace and mercy. The secret of maintaining right judgment is found here: Treat others as you would have them treat you. Treat them with understanding, compassion, and love. Knowing how much we need mercy, we can extend mercy to others. If we are aware of our own sins and of the potential for evil in ourselves, we will not be so quick to judge others harshly and without pity. The way of Christ is a humble way.

6

A Narrow Way

The royal way is a narrow way. In Matthew 7:13-29 and Luke 6:46-49 Jesus described for his listeners a hard way that leads to life, a way entered through a narrow gate.

"Enter by the narrow gate; for the gate is wide and the way is easy, that leads to destruction, and those who enter by it are many. For the gate is narrow and the way is hard, that leads to life, and those who find it are few" (Matthew 7:13-14).

This passage begins the conclusion of Jesus' Sermon on the Mount and Sermon on the Plain. Both sermons call Jesus' listeners to make a decision. Jesus called his listeners to walk the narrow road to the kingdom of God. But he said the door to the Kingdom is small. Only a few enter it. The rest go another way, a way that *seems* right but is actually a way of illusion. This other way is popular and appealing because no cost, no commitment are involved.

A writer of proverbs once observed that a way that seems right to people ends in death (Proverbs 14:12). Jesus says in our lesson that the broad way is death. Only the narrow way is life, and Jesus is the narrow way.

Some people dislike hearing Christians talk of Jesus in what seems to be exclusive terms. But while talking with his disciples the week before his death, Jesus said, "I am the way, and the truth, and the life; no one comes to the Father, but by me" (John 14:6). This statement of Jesus is a foundation of Christian teaching.

In Jesus Christ the mighty God is revealed in a totally unique way. Our conviction as Christians is that this same Jesus is the Messiah of Israel. Historically the church always has joined with the apostolic witness: "There is salvation in no one else, for there is no other name under heaven given among men by which we must be saved" (Acts 4:12).

This emphasis of Jesus sounds a great deal like Psalm 1.

"Blessed is the man
who walks not in the counsel of the wicked,
nor stands in the way of sinners,
nor sits in the seat of scoffers;
but his delight is in the law of the LORD,
and on his law he meditates day and night.
He is like a tree
planted by streams of water,
that yields fruit in its season,
and its leaf does not wither.
In all that he does, he prospers" (Psalm 1:1-3).

The person who avoids evil counsel and bad companions is truly blessed. This righteous person delights in God's Word instead, and like a hearty tree produces good things. Such a person's life becomes filled with purpose and peace. Persons who side with the voices of scorn and ridicule are doomed to failure. Because these persons are rootless and filled with greed, their lives amount to little in God's sight. Judgment is their lot, not happiness. Therefore, those who read Psalm 1 are called to choose between these two ways of life.

The narrow way is the way of total commitment to the saving grace of Jesus Christ. The narrow way is likewise commitment to the teachings and lifestyle of Jesus. Such a confession, such a commitment, cannot be held in arrogance. Indeed, Christ came to a needy humanity. He is the property of no one, not even his church.

All the church does is announce the goodness and mercy of God through God's Son. We are witnesses to what God has done and is doing. Ours is a humble witness to the gospel of reconciliation. We speak to others as one beggar to another beggar, sharing where to go to get bread.

The ideas of "broad" and "narrow" seem to relate to the ways the people took Jesus' teachings. His way must have seemed narrow indeed to the people of his time. The same is true today. But this idea is a mistake. Jesus sets us free!

The Old Testament spoke of the coming day when a great "light" would shine upon Israel. This coming of the Messiah would be a period of great joy and enthusiasm for the people of God. In fact, the repentant nation would become a witness to the Messiah's reign, and peace would dominate the affairs of people.

The New Testament tells of Jesus bringing salvation to the people. It tells of Jesus producing joy, giving a right mind, and releasing the spirits of persons from the bondage of selfishness. Jesus' way brings the abundant life, a life that causes songs of joy to well up in our hearts.

And best of all, these experiences are not pushed off into the distant future. They are the blessings of the people right now. To speak of eternal life in the presence of God is but another chapter in the almost unbelievable story of God's love. This hardly sounds like lifeless and drab legalism. No long face here, but a jubilant spirit rejoices in the goodness of the Lord in the land of the living.

Tragic beyond imagination is the idea that Jesus' vitality and excellence should be seen as restrictive or as crushingly narrow. Certainly the broad way is no easier way. Not at all!

Look how hard we work for money, which brings little satisfaction. Look how we run after entertainment and relaxation but find little value in them. We go to school for years but are not smart enough to bring peace to a small town, much less to the world. Look how we willingly sacrifice our health and even our families to get ahead in the business or social world.

For all that effort we are no closer to answering the question of why we were born in the first place or what our sacrifices will mean in the long run. Am I exaggerating? Look carefully at life in the world around you, if not your own life, and see if this is the truth or not.

Do not compare Jesus' teachings to the life of the institutional church. Compare the church to the teachings of Jesus. Jesus makes us free, forgives us over and over again, and gives us real life and makes that life beautiful.

The church's failure to model such a life of triumph is not a failure of the gospel. The church is being purged by the Lord himself. The church is the community that professes its sinfulness and its need of grace. Of course, the church makes mistakes, even occasional tragic blunders. But the church is not the Savior. The church is itself being saved!

Thank God some churches are wonderfully alive, filled with the spirit of reverence and obedience. People in these churches have discovered that Jesus liberates. To be in worship services in these churches is glorious. The narrow way has opened for them the door to a land of happiness that nothing can overcome. Ultimately the broad way is really a narrow way, because it does not make good on its promises and leaves people battered, sour, and needlessly dead.

We are talking here about what Paul called the

"crucified" life, the life of joy through self-denial. To the Galatians Paul wrote, "I have been crucified with Christ; it is no longer I who live, but Christ who lives in me; and the life I now live in the flesh I live by faith in the Son of God, who loved me and gave himself for me" (Galatians 2:20).

This may seem puzzling. To allow the interests of Christ to control one's life would seem at first to deny one's individuality and freedom. But it is quite the reverse.

Acknowledging Christ as the Savior and Lord of one's life sets one free to develop in ways that benefit the individual and society. God wants to make people over again, to free them from the control of selfishness and release them to live a satisfying life of selflessness. Jesus helps us grow in love and service to God and the world.

At another time Jesus said, "If any man would come after me, let him deny himself and take up his cross and follow me. For whoever would save his life will lose it, and whoever loses his life for my sake will find it" (Matthew 16:24-25).

Being a follower of the Lord, leaving self-interest behind, and taking up one's cross are all characteristics of the life to which Jesus calls us. In calling us to this kind of life, Jesus helps us find our true self. And that is real freedom.

The Christian faith is concerned not only with right experience but with right belief. Both the Old Testament and the New Testament agree that it is not only important *that* one believes but *what* one believes. The next part of Jesus' sermon warned his listeners, "Beware of false prophets, who come to you in sheep's clothing but inwardly are ravenous wolves" (Matthew 7:15).

The shadows of false prophets loomed large in Israel's past. False prophets caused the children of Israel much misery as these false teachers challenged not only the message of the Old Testament prophets of God but even the authority of God.

The ministry of the apostle Paul was plagued by

false apostles (2 Corinthians 11:1-29) and erroneous teachings (Colossians 2:8-23). Paul instructed young Timothy to beware of false teachers (1 Timothy 1:3-7). Similar warnings are found in 2 Peter 2:1-3; 1 John 2:18 (against the antichrists); and Jude 3-4. These false teachers attacked the early church's commitments to the messiahship of Jesus and Jesus' resurrection from the dead.

The Sermon on the Mount describes three groups of people. First are those who are eager to do God's will. These are the people who listen to what Jesus says and then follow through by doing it. These are the ones who live out the meaning of the Beatitudes and therefore are in line with the Old Testament prophets, the true prophets. "Rejoice and be glad, for your reward is great in heaven, for so men persecuted the prophets who were before you" (Matthew 5:12).

Second are those who are shallow in their faith, who muddle things a bit but generally make good citizens. In this category are those teachers who do not interpret the Law faithfully (Matthew 5:19), the self-righteous (6:1-7, 16-18), and the judgmental (7:1-5).

Third are those who are hostile to the gospel and hinder God's will at every turn. Among these are the accusers (Matthew 5:11-12), the enemies (5:43-48), those bold in their sins (7:6), and those mentioned in the Scripture for this chapter, the false teachers (7:15-20).

As believers we are to treat members of the spiritual family with love. We are to treat with mercy those outside the faith who are sympathetic or at least tolerant. Those who are openly hostile we are to treat with caution.

But the false teachers of whom Jesus spoke are not so easy to identify. They look and act so much like everyone else. These are the people who look perfectly harmless and even helpful but are deceivers in their hearts and at times malicious. These false teachers look quite authentic and in fact have even used Christ's name to do wonderful things. But in the final analysis they are unknown by the Christ in whose name they profess to speak.

We cannot make quick decisions about false teachers, and we cannot take Jesus' words to sanction a witch hunt in the church. Jesus told us that the false teachers' works betray their intentions. Determining the nature of one's works takes time. We cannot tell at a glance whether a tree will produce good fruit or bad fruit. But it will produce sooner or later. At the last judgment, if not before, false teachers will be turned away from the Kingdom by the Lord himself. "Not every one who says to me, 'Lord, Lord,' shall enter the kingdom of heaven, but he who does the will of my Father who is in heaven. On that day many will say to me, 'Lord, Lord, did we not prophesy in your name, and cast out demons in your name, and do many mighty works in your name?' And then will I declare to them, 'I never knew you; depart from me, you evildoers' " (Matthew 7:21-23).

Jesus told his disciples that they would recognize false teachers for what they were—wolves in sheep's clothing (Matthew 7:15). The Lord did not tell us exactly what to do about such false teachers, although Jesus was confident God would deal justly with them. The mood of the text suggests that we are not to listen to obviously false leaders if we are to remain faithful to Jesus.

However, such discernment must not be harsh and unloving. We have already been warned by Jesus against that danger in the section on judging others (Matthew 7:1-5).

We are to be cautious, especially where new Christians are concerned. We Christians must learn what the Scripture teaches about God's will so that we can know the mind and heart of the Savior after whom we are named.

Most people seem to want life without a cross, security without risk, and happiness without pain. But life does not work that way, not in a world partially shaped by evil influences. Suffering actually may be an important way to discover meaning in life.

The crowd that heard Jesus preach the Sermon on the Mount understood something of suffering and privation.

One of the striking qualities of the Sermon on the Mount and the Sermon on the Plain is that Jesus did not rush in and promise the people who heard him immediate deliverance from their problems. He did not tell them that their physical lives would be different. He did not tell them that life would be easy, free of problems, or free from suffering.

He did offer them the Kingdom, but he hinted that they could find fulfillment in their powerlessness if they listened to his message and took it to heart. Their lives would change from the inside out. They would look at life in a different way.

Jesus did not try to make the poor satisfied with the ways they were being exploited. Not at all. But he taught them that they did not have to live in bitterness while they were waiting for the inevitable overthrow of a selfish and manipulative social order. Jesus really believed that God was preparing something great for the little people, perhaps at the expense of the big people.

In the Lord's Prayer Jesus asked that God's will would be done on earth as it is being done in heaven (Matthew 6:10). This means God's will is done perfectly in heaven. And heaven is where we want to go in due time, because going there will open us to unimaginable love.

The perfect will of God can also be done on earth, though considerable barriers will need to be overcome. Not the least of these barriers are our own cloudy understandings of the divine will and our lapses from a zealous spiritual life. Of course, we must contend always with those spiritual powers that delight in distorting God's will and discouraging people from seeking it.

When Jesus called his disciples, they did not understand all that call would mean. That is true for us as well. I did not know myself that Jesus was going to lead me in ways that called many of my values into question. I only knew at first that I had been accepted by God and that I wanted to witness wherever I could to what had happened in my life.

We may never know what Jesus' disciples felt in their hearts when they first heard these sayings. But I am sure that they were aghast as it gradually dawned on them that this man who spoke to them would settle for nothing less than total commitment to his way. I too felt—and still feel—the inner wrenching of my heart as some new demand of Jesus calls me back to the central truth of the gospel: All of us who want to be Christian must find our identity only in Jesus, the Christ of God.

So we look to Jesus our living Lord to lead us to God's will, which is to love God and to love others with every ounce of energy in us. At first we may pull back a bit from such radical commitment. But our hesitancy is a sure sign that we are not serious about following him. If hesitancy becomes habit, then our intention to live a spiritual life is at an end. We must say to God and ourselves, "Here I am. I know I cannot turn back. Help me. I am weak." This prayer can be the entrance into the *life* of faith and love. Jesus gave these sayings in the Sermon on the Mount to lead us into this abundant life.

If doubts and fears arise, as they most surely will, plunge them repeatedly into God's love. God has called you to become fully human, and God will not fail you. Remember that despair is an enemy. Chase it away with joy. Submit your reasonings to faith. Learn to see God's kindness where others do not see it. Learn to be still and to meditate on the Scripture, especially those passages that tell you about the life of Jesus Christ.

If a teaching from the Sermon on the Mount seems too hard for you, remember who is guiding you. He is the Christ of God, who lovingly surrendered himself to misunderstanding, brutality, and death for our sake. Follow him. He will set you free. He will lead you into the Kingdom of his love, and there you will have rest.

Jesus said, "Every one then who hears these words of mine and does them will be like a wise man who built his house upon the rock; and the rain fell, and the floods came, and the winds blew and beat upon that house, but it did not fall, because it had been founded on the rock. And every one who hears these words of mine and does not do them will be like a foolish man who built his house upon the sand; and the rain fell, and the floods came, and the winds blew and beat against that house, and it fell; and great was the fall of it" (Matthew 7:24-27).

The sermons of Jesus, particularly the Sermon on the Mount, contain so many spiritual treasures. To mine them all is quite beyond me. If this study contains any salvation, it is in the common fire between our hearts, the fire that seeks out God, burning for God. May God go with you, pilgrim in the royal way. May God be exalted in your heart and life and in mine.